by Iain Gray

LangSyne

PUBLISHING

WRITING *to* REMEMBER

LangSyne

PUBLISHING

WRITING *to* REMEMBER

79 Main Street, Newtongrange,
Midlothian EH22 4NA
Tel: 0131 344 0414   Fax: 0845 075 6085
E-mail: info@lang-syne.co.uk
www.langsyneshop.co.uk

Design by Dorothy Meikle
Printed by Printwell Ltd
© Lang Syne Publishers Ltd 2019

ISBN 978-1-85217-534-4

Morgan

MOTTO:
As I live, I hope
(and)
Fortune favours the bold.

CREST:
The head of a reindeer.

NAME variations include:
Morgaine
Morgan
Morgrain

Chapter one:

The origins of popular surnames

by George Forbes and Iain Gray

If you don't know where you came from, you won't know where you're going is a frequently quoted observation and one that has a particular resonance today when there has been a marked upsurge in interest in genealogy, with increasing numbers of people curious to trace their family roots.

Main sources for genealogical research include census returns and official records of births, marriages and deaths – and the key to unlocking the detail they contain is obviously a family surname, one that has been 'inherited' and passed from generation to generation.

No matter our station in life, we all have a surname – but it was not until about the middle of the fourteenth century that the practice of being identified by a particular surname became commonly established throughout the British Isles.

Previous to this, it was normal for a person to be identified through the use of only a forename.

But as population gradually increased and there were many more people with the same forename, surnames were adopted to distinguish one person, or community, from another.

Many common English surnames are patronymic in origin, meaning they stem from the forename of one's father – with 'Johnson,' for example, indicating 'son of John.'

It was the Normans, in the wake of their eleventh century conquest of Anglo-Saxon England, a pivotal moment in the nation's history, who first brought surnames into usage – although it was a gradual process.

For the Normans, these were names initially based on the title of their estates, local villages and chateaux in France to distinguish and identify these landholdings.

Such grand descriptions also helped enhance the prestige of these warlords and generally glorify their lofty positions high above the humble serfs slaving away below in the pecking order who had only single names, often with Biblical connotations as in Pierre and Jacques.

The only descriptive distinctions among the peasantry concerned their occupations, like 'Pierre the swineherd' or 'Jacques the ferryman.'

Roots of surnames that came into usage in England not only included Norman-French, but also Old French, Old Norse, Old English, Middle English, German, Latin, Greek, Hebrew and the Gaelic languages of the Celts.

The Normans themselves were originally Vikings, or 'Northmen', who raided, colonised and eventually settled down around the French coastline.

The had sailed up the Seine in their longboats in 900AD under their ferocious leader Rollo and ruled the roost in north eastern France before sailing over to conquer England in 1066 under Duke William of Normandy – better known to posterity as William the Conqueror, or King William I of England.

Granted lands in the newly-conquered England, some of their descendants later acquired territories in Wales, Scotland and Ireland – taking not only their own surnames, but also the practice of adopting a surname, with them.

But it was in England where Norman rule and custom first impacted, particularly in relation to the adoption of surnames.

This is reflected in the famous *Domesday Book*, a massive survey of much of England and Wales, ordered by William I, to determine who owned what, what it was worth and therefore how much they were liable to pay in taxes to the voracious Royal Exchequer.

Completed in 1086 and now held in the National Archives in Kew, London, 'Domesday' was an Old English word meaning 'Day of Judgement.'

This was because, in the words of one contemporary chronicler, "its decisions, like those of the Last Judgement, are unalterable."

It had been a requirement of all those English landholders – from the richest to the poorest – that they identify themselves for the purposes of the survey and for future reference by means of a surname.

This is why the *Domesday Book*, although written in Latin as was the practice for several centuries with both civic and ecclesiastical records, is an invaluable source for the early appearance of a wide range of English surnames.

Several of these names were coined in connection with occupations.

These include Baker and Smith, while Cooks, Chamberlains, Constables and Porters were to be found carrying out duties in large medieval households.

The church's influence can be found in names such as Bishop, Friar and Monk while the popular name of Bennett derives from the late fifth to mid-sixth century Saint Benedict, founder of the Benedictine order of monks.

The early medical profession is represented by Barber, while businessmen produced names that include Merchant and Sellers.

Down at the village watermill, the names that cropped up included Millar/Miller, Walker and Fuller, while other self-explanatory trades included Cooper, Tailor, Mason and Wright.

Even the scenery was utilised as in Moor, Hill, Wood and Forrest – while the hunt and the chase supplied names that include Hunter, Falconer, Fowler and Fox.

Colours are also a source of popular surnames, as in Black, Brown, Gray/Grey, Green and White, and would have denoted the colour of the clothing the person habitually wore or, apart from the obvious exception of 'Green', one's hair colouring or even complexion.

The surname Red developed into Reid, while

Blue was rare and no-one wanted to be associated with yellow.

Rather self-important individuals took surnames that include Goodman and Wiseman, while physical attributes crept into surnames such as Small and Little.

Many families proudly boast the heraldic device known as a Coat of Arms, as featured on our front cover.

The central motif of the Coat of Arms would originally have been what was borne on the shield of a warrior to distinguish himself from others on the battlefield.

Not featured on the Coat of Arms, but highlighted on page three, is the family motto and related crest – with the latter frequently different from the central motif.

Adding further variety to the rich cultural heritage that is represented by surnames is the appearance in recent times in lists of the 100 most common names found in England of ones that include Khan, Patel and Singh – names that have proud roots in the vast sub-continent of India.

Echoes of a far distant past can still be found in our surnames and they can be borne with pride in commemoration of our forebears.

Chapter two:

Myth and magic

A name whose origins stretch back through the dim mists of time, 'Morgan' is ranked 37th in some lists of the 100 most common surnames in England, although it is particularly identified with Wales.

Derived from the Welsh personal name 'Morcant', with 'mor' indicating 'sea' and 'cant' indicating 'circle', some sources also assert it may have originally denoted 'great kingdom.'

Of ancient Celtic roots, it is steeped in myth and magic – lending itself as it does to the goddess Morgan, also known as Morrigan, Morrigu or Morrighan.

Known as "The Phantom Queen" or "Great Queen", this Mother Goddess was not only recognised as a fertility goddess but also as a goddess of war, sovereignty, water and magic.

Said to be a shape-shifter, typically taking on the guise of a crow, she was also what is known as a Triple Goddess – able to take on at will the aspects of Maiden, Mother and Crone.

Her name first appears in the twelfth century Welsh cleric Geoffrey of Monmouth's *Vita Merlin – Life of Merlin* – which formed the colourful basis for subsequent Arthurian legends that feature the mysterious Lady of the Lake and the sorceress Morgana le Fay.

Interestingly, to this day the magical creatures known as water sprites are known in Welsh as 'morgans', while Glamorganshire is said to have been the home of King Arthur, who was of the Royal House of Morgan.

Flowing through the veins of many bearers of the name today is the blood of those ancient Britons who became the subject of myth and legend.

Of Celtic pedigree, these early inhabitants of the British Isles were settled for centuries from a line south of the River Forth in Scotland all the way down to the south coast of England and with a particular presence in Wales.

Speaking a Celtic language known as Brythonic, they boasted a glorious culture that flourished even after the Roman invasion of Britain in 43 AD and the subsequent consolidation of Roman power by about 84 AD.

With many of the original Britons absorbing

aspects of Roman culture, they became 'Romano-British' – while still retaining their own proud Celtic heritage.

Following the withdrawal of the last Roman legions from Britain in 406, what is now modern-day Wales, or *Cymru*, fragmented into a number of independent kingdoms – with the most powerful king being recognised as overall ruler.

Recognised as King of the Britons, he had to battle with not only internal rivals but also the depredations of the wild sea rovers known as the Vikings, or Northmen.

There were also the Anglo-Saxons to contend with – as those Germanic tribes who invaded and settled in the south and east of the island of Britain from about the early fifth century were known.

These Anglo-Saxons were composed of the Jutes, from the area of the Jutland Peninsula in modern Denmark, the Saxons from Lower Saxony, in modern Germany and the Angles from the Angeln area of Germany.

It was the Angles who gave the name 'Engla land', or 'Aengla land' – better known as 'England.'

They held sway in what became England from approximately 550 to 1066, with the main kingdoms those of Sussex, Wessex, Northumbria, Mercia, Kent, East Anglia and Essex.

Whoever controlled the most powerful of these kingdoms was tacitly recognised as overall 'king' – one of the most noted being Alfred the Great, King of Wessex from 871 to 899.

The Anglo-Saxons, meanwhile, had usurped the power of the indigenous Britons, such as those found in Wales, and who referred to them as 'Saeson' or 'Saxones.'

It is from this that the Scottish Gaelic term for 'English people' of 'Sasannach' derives, the Irish Gaelic 'Sasanach' and the Welsh 'Saeson.'

The death knell of Anglo-Saxon supremacy and also what remained of Welsh independence was sounded with the Norman Conquest and the defeat of Harold II, the last of the Anglo-Saxon monarchs, at the battle of Hastings.

Within an astonishingly short space of time, Norman manners, customs and law were imposed on England – laying the basis for what subsequently became established 'English' custom and practice.

In 1282, by which time most of Wales had come under Anglo-Norman rule, final rebellion against this was crushed by England's Edward I, and it is from this date that the heir apparent to the British throne has borne the title of Prince of Wales.

An abortive rebellion was led in the early fifteenth century by the freedom fighter Owain Glyndŵr, while in the following century, under Henry VIII, Wales was 'incorporated' into the English kingdom; in 1707, in common with Scotland, Wales became part of the United Kingdom.

Chapter three:

Intrigue and piracy

The Morgan name is one that features prominently in the frequently turbulent historical record.

Born in 1546 in Llantarnam, a member of a prominent Monmouthshire family of Morgans, Thomas Morgan was the Welsh confidante and secretary of the ill-fated Mary, Queen of Scots who was involved in a complex but ultimately abortive plot to assassinate England's Queen Elizabeth I.

The unsuspecting Mary knew nothing of the plot, but nevertheless was executed at Fotheringhay Castle, Northamptonshire in 1587 for her alleged complicity in it.

A staunch Roman Catholic, Morgan had been employed for a time as Secretary of the Archbishop of York and then with Lord Shrewsbury, who had the Scots Queen in his care for a time.

Mary had sought refuge in England and the protection of her cousin Elizabeth after being deposed from the Scottish throne and her defeat at the battle of Langside, near Glasgow, in 1568.

But, fearing that she may have become the

focal point for plots against her, Elizabeth on the advice of her advisors had Mary placed in captivity under the care of a number of her trusted noblemen.

It was while she was in the care of Lord Shrewsbury that Mary made the acquaintance of Morgan – who, because of his Catholic faith, was taken into her confidence and employed as her trusted secretary and general go-between with her sympathisers and supporters.

Part of Morgan's duties involved secretly delivering letters from Mary to her supporters in the French royal court, and it was while on such a mission that, along with the Catholic Dr William Parry, he hatched a plot to kill Elizabeth.

This became known to posterity as the Babington Plot, because it also involved the young English nobleman Anthony Babington.

But the complex plot was thwarted thanks to the efforts of Francis Walsingham, chief of Elizabeth's intelligence service, and who controlled not only a network of spies and double-agents but also the skills of his code-breaker Thomas Phelippes – who was able to decipher the plotters' coded communications.

The plotters were arrested when their murderous plan came to light and the conspirators, including Babington and Dr William Parry were executed through the horrific ordeal of being hanged, drawn and quartered.

Morgan escaped the executioner because he had been able to flee to France – but he was clapped in irons for a time in the Bastille in Paris on suspicion by some of Mary's supporters that he had actually been working as a double- agent for Walsingham.

Released on the personal orders of the Pope, he died in Amiens in 1603 – the main agent of a plot that had tragic consequences for Mary, Queen of Scots.

One interesting footnote, meanwhile, is that the character of the great spymaster Francis Walsingham is thought to have been one of the inspirations for Ian Fleming's character of 'M' in his James Bond novels.

On the high seas, one particularly infamous bearer of the Morgan name was the English Royal Navy admiral, privateer and pirate Sir Henry Morgan.

Born in 1635 in Llanrumney Hall, near Cardiff, the son of a Welsh country squire, he gained a feared reputation as one of the most ruthless pirates on the Spanish Main.

Little is known of his early life, but it is

known that he commanded a vessel in late 1655 that, with the approval of the English government, seized the Spanish-held islands of Providencia, Colombia and Santa Catalina.

With the government happy to acquiesce to Morgan's plundering of Spanish vessels and territories, he roved the high seas – capturing the fortress of San Lorenzo on the coast of Panama in December of 1670 and slaughtering 300 of its Spanish garrison.

Later capturing the city of Panama itself and torturing its inhabitants in a feverish search for gold, Morgan and his blood-thirsty crew sacked the city to such an extent that it had to be completely rebuilt later on a new site several kilometres to the west.

The sack of Panama had violated a 1670 peace treaty and Morgan was arrested and taken back to England to face the consequences.

But, claiming he had been unaware of the treaty, instead of being punished he was actually knighted and, fourteen years before his death in 1688, appointed to the powerful and lucrative post of Lieutenant Governor of Jamaica.

He has since been immortalised in a number of books and films, notably the 1935 *Captain Blood*, starring a swashbuckling Errol Flynn and adapted from a novel by Rafael Sabatini.

A noted bearer of the name who pursued decidedly more peaceful pursuits was the immensely wealthy American banker, financier, art collector and philanthropist John Pierpont Morgan, better known as J.P. Morgan.

Born in 1837 in Hartford, Connecticut into a wealthy banking family and working for a number of years for the family business, in 1871 he co-founded with Anthony J. Drexel the banking firm of Drexel, Morgan and Company – renamed J.P. Morgan and Company following the death of Drexel 24 years later.

One of his biggest financial successes was the creation of the giant United States Steel Corporation, formed through his financing of the Federal Steel Company and its merger with a number of other iron and steel companies in 1901.

Another of his many business interests was the International Mercantile Marine Company, one of whose subsidiaries was the White Star Line – operator of the ill-fated liner *Titanic* that sank on her maiden voyage to New York in 1912 after colliding with an iceberg in the mid-Atlantic and with the loss of 1,635 passengers and crew.

J.P. Morgan, in Europe at the time, had been scheduled to travel on the doomed liner, but cancelled at the last minute.

Following the tragedy, he said: "Monetary losses amount to nothing in life. It is the loss of life that counts."

A collector of paintings, books, clocks and a number of other valuable works of art and a generous benefactor of institutions that include the American Museum of Natural History, Harvard University and the Metropolitan Museum of Art, he died in 1913.

In the world of contemporary politics, Hywel Rhodri Morgan, better known as Rhodri Morgan, is the prominent Welsh Labour Party politician born in Cardiff in 1939.

A graduate in politics, philosophy and economics from St John's College, Oxford he was elected Member of Parliament (MP) for Cardiff West in 1987 – and went on to hold high level posts that include Shadow Environment Spokesman and chairman of the House of Commons Select Committee on Public Administration.

He is best known, however, as First Secretary, then First Minister, for Wales from 2000 to 2009 in the Welsh Assembly.

In the ecclesiastical realm, Barry Cennydd Morgan, born in 1947 in Gwaun-Cae-Gurwen, Neath has served as Archbishop of Wales since 2003.

Ordained as a priest in 1972 and the author of a number of books that include the one on the poetry of R.S. Thomas, he was appointed Patron of the Welsh Language in 2013, while he is also a former president of the Welsh Centre for International Affairs.

Chapter four:

On the world stage

Born in 1915 in Detroit, Michigan, Harry Bratsberg was the American actor, director and writer better known by his stage name of Harry Morgan.

Of Swedish and Norwegian ancestry, he first took to the stage in 1937, making his screen debut in the 1942 war film *The Shores of Tripoli*.

Other big screen credits include the 1943 *The Ox-Bow Incident*, the 1954 *The Glenn Miller Story*, the 1969 *Support Your Local Sheriff* and, from 1976, *The Shootist*.

He is best known, however, for his role of Colonel Sherman T. Potter in the popular 1975 to 1983 television series *M*A*S*H*, while other television credits include *Dragnet*, *Gunsmoke* and *Have Gun – Will Travel*.

An inductee of the Hall of Fame of Great Western Performers, he died in 2011.

On British shores, **Colin Morgan**, born in 1986 in Armagh, is the Northern Irish actor known for playing the title role in the 2008 to 2012 BBC television series *Merlin* and for which he won a National Television Award.

Born in Dublin in 1952, **Dermot Morgan** was the Irish comedian and actor best known for his role of Father Ted Crilly in the television sitcom *Father Ted*, which ran for three series from 1995.

A schoolteacher before he embarked on his career as a comedian and actor, he was also known for his part in the Irish television show *The Live Mike* and the radio comedy show *Scrap Saturday*.

The recipient of a BAFTA Award for Best Actor for his role in *Father Ted*, he died in 1998.

Back on American shores, **Jeffrey Dean Morgan**, born in Seattle in 1966, is the actor of television and film best known for his role of Denny Duquette in the 2005 medical drama *Grey's Anatomy*.

Other television credits include *ER*, *Monk* and, from 2012, *Magic City*, while big screen credits include the 1999 *Road Kill*, the 2006 *Jam*, the 2008 *Days of Wrath* and, from 2012, *Red Dawn*.

Born in Chicago in 1986, **Trevor Morgan** is the American actor who, after appearing in a number of television commercials, has gone on to gain big screen credits that include the 2000 *A Rumor of*

Angels and *Jurassic Park II*, the 2003 *Uncle Nino* and the 2010 *Brotherhood*.

Known for his role of Klaus Mikaelson in the television series *The Vampire Diaries*, Joseph Martin, better known by his stage name of **Joseph Morgan**, is the English actor born in London in 1981.

Nominated in both 2011 and 2012 for the Teen Choice Award for Choice TV Villain for his role in *The Vampire Diaries*, his big screen credits include the 2003 *Henry VIII*, the 2007 *Mansfield Park* and the 2011 *The Immortals*.

Born in New York City in 1880, Francis Phillip Wuppermann was the birth name of the American actor **Frank Morgan**, best known for having played five separate roles – including the title role – in the 1939 *The Wizard of Oz*.

In addition to the role of Wizard, he played the carnival huckster Professor Marvel, the Gatekeeper of the Enchanted City, the Coachman of the carriage drawn by The Horse of a Different Color and the Doorman leading to the Wizard's Hall.

With other major film credits that include the 1936 *The Great Ziegfeld*, the 1938 *Paradise for Three* and the 1948 *The Three Musketeers* and the recipient of two stars on the Hollywood Walk of Fame, he died in 1949.

Born in 1981 in Calgary, Alberta, **Michelle Morgan** is the Canadian television and film actress and singer known for her role in the television series *Heartland*, while big screen credits include the 2008 horror film *Diary of the Dead*.

Known as "The Queen of Laughter" and "The Queen of Comedy", **Gladys Morgan** was the renowned Welsh comedienne of stage and radio born in 1893 in Swansea.

First performing as part of an act called The Three Virgins, she later dropped her broad Welsh accent in favour of a Lancashire one.

Before this, she had teamed up with fellow comedian Frank Laurie, whom she married, and the couple had a successful double act with Morgan as the comedian and her husband as the straight-man.

The couple worked during the Second World War for ENSA – the Entertainment National Service Association – and were regulars on the popular radio programme *Workers Playtime*.

One of her quips from this period of strict wartime rationing and austerity was: "I gave the lodger a boiled egg for breakfast. Me and the kids had egg soup."

Known for her toothless, infectious laugh

and trademark striped blazer and a regular on the variety circuit during the 1960s, she died in 1983.

Behind the camera lens Elaine Floyd, better known by her married name of **Elaine Morgan**, born in 1920 in Hopkinstown, near Pontypridd, is the Welsh television writer and author who has written for series that include the 1975 *How Green Was My Valley*, adapted from the book of the name, the 1979 *Testament of Youth* and, from 1981, *The Life and Times of David Lloyd George*.

The recipient of two BAFTA awards and two Writers' Guild Awards, she is also the author of an evolutionary anthropology series of books that include *The Descent of Woman*, *The Aquatic Ape* and *The Naked Darwinist*.

Also the recipient of an OBE, she was the mother of **John Dylan Morgan**, the physicist, hypnotherapist and author born in Burnley, Lancashire in 1946; author of the acclaimed 1986 *Principles of Hypnotherapy*, he died in 2011.

Born in Philadelphia in 1854, **George Morgan** was the actor and prolific screenwriter whose many writing credits include the 1914 *The Dilemma*, the 1922 *The Hurricane Express* and, screened a year after his death in 1936, *Dick Tracy*.

In contemporary times, **Peter Morgan**, born in London in 1963, is the British film writer and playwright whose television credits include the 2003 *Henry VIII*, the 2006 *Longford* and the 2010 *The Special* Relationship.

Big screen credits include the 2006 *The Last King of Scotland* – for which he and co-writer Jeremy Brook won a BAFTA Film Award – the 2008 *Frost/Nixon* and the 2011 *Tinker, Tailor, Soldier, Spy*.

Born in 1965 in Guildford, **Piers Morgan** is the British journalist and television host who was born Piers Stefan O'Meara.

After working as editor of the show business column for the *Sun* tabloid newspaper, he was appointed editor of the former *News of the World* newspaper by its proprietor Rupert Murdoch when aged only 28.

Later appointed editor of the *Daily Mirror*, he was sacked from the post in 2004 after the newspaper published what turned out to be faked photographs of Iraqi prisoners being abused by British troops – although Morgan was unaware at the time that the controversial photographs had been faked.

Now pursuing a highly successful television career, including host of CNN's *Piers Morgan Live*, he is also the author of a number of autobiographical works that include his 2005 T*he Insider: The Private Diaries of a Scandalous Decade* and the 2009 *God Bless America: Misadventures of a Big Mouth Brit*.

Bearers of the Morgan name have also excelled in the highly competitive world of sport.

On the water, **John Morgan**, born in 1930, is the American former sailor who won the gold medal in the 6-metre class event at the 1952 Olympics in Sydney.

In the rough and tumble that is the game of rugby union, **Kevin Morgan**, born in 1977 in Pontypridd, is the Welsh full-back and wing who, in addition to playing for teams that include Pontypridd, Swansea, Celtic Warriors and Neath, at the time of writing has won 48 caps playing for his country.

Born in London in 1985, Oliver Morgan, better known as **Olly Morgan**, is the full-back who has played for Gloucester and, at the time of writing, has won two caps playing for England.

Born in 1884 in Haverfordwest, **Ivor Morgan** was the Welsh forward who played for both Swansea and Glamorgan and won 13 caps playing for his country between 1908 and 1914; he died in 1943.

On the fields of football – or soccer as it is known in North America – Alexandra Morgan, better known as **Alex Morgan**, is the forward who was a member of the gold medal-winning U.S. women's team at the 2012 Olympics in London.

Born in 1989, she has played for clubs in the National Women's Soccer League that include Western New York Flash.

On the tennis court, **George Morgan**, born in 1993 in Bolton, is the British tennis player who, along with Mate Pavić, won the Boys' Doubles title at the 2011 Wimbledon Championships.

Born in Dublin in 1986, **Eoin Morgan** is the Irish cricketer who, in addition to playing for clubs that include Middlesex, has also played for both the Ireland and England national teams.

The recipient of an OBE for his services to cricket, **Frederick Morgan**, born in 1937 in Tredegar, Wales is the former president of the International Cricket Council (ICC), who has also held other administrative posts that include chairman of the England and Wales Cricket Board and Glamorgan County Cricket Club.

From cricket to weightlifting, **Dave Morgan**, born in 1964, is the Welsh weightlifter who, at the

1982 Commonwealth Games in Brisbane, became the games' youngest ever weightlifting champion.

In the world of music, **George Morgan** was the American country music singer best known for top-selling albums that include his 1964 T*ender Lovin Care*, the 1969 *Like a Bird* and, from 1971, *Real George*. Born in 1924 in Waverly, Tennessee and an inductee of the Country Music Hall of Fame, he died in 1975.

He was the father of Loretta Lynn Morgan, born in 1959 in Nashville and better known as the country music singer **Lorrie Morgan**, and who has enjoyed hit albums that include her 1989 *Leave the Light On* and the 2009 *A Moment in Time*.

In the creative world of the written word, **Edwin Morgan** was the distinguished Scottish poet who, in 2004, was named as the first Scots Maker, as the officially recognised national poet is now known.

Born in Glasgow in 1920 and growing up in nearby Rutherglen, he is famed for a number of poems that include his 1968 *The Billy Boys* and the 1977 *A Good Year for Death*, while his *Collected Poems* was published in 1990.

One of his last works, *Poem for the Opening of the Scottish Parliament*, was read out at the opening of the Parliament building in Edinburgh in October of 2004 by fellow poet Liz Lochead, who succeeded him as Scots Makar following his death in 2010.

One particularly flamboyant bearer of the proud name of Morgan was the English expert on etiquette and manners **Anthony John Morgan**, born in 1959 in Sunderland, Tyne on Wear. The son of an employee of Scottish Shell, he grew up near the town of Perth before studying at Cheltenham Art College.

Style editor for a time with the *Gentleman's Magazine (GQ)*, he is best known for his *Morgan's Manners* Saturday column in *The Times* newspaper, in which he often described good manners as "the path of least offence."

He would offer sage advice for readers who wrote in to enquire about such diverse topics as which piece of cutlery to use at a dinner party and how to hold it and how to properly interact with one's host.

Also the author of the 1996 *Debrett's Etiquette and Modern Manners*, he was known to have proudly possessed before his death in 2000 sixty made-to-measure Savile Row Suits, ninety pairs of shoes and 300 monogrammed shirts, while he also took great pride in cashing his cheques in London's upmarket Claridge's Hotel.